God bless you ♡ W9-AVZ-911
as you go onto further
study. May this
little book become a
companion with your
Bible. —

God bless you
bunches,

Aunt Laura + Uncle Lloyd

1995

The Secret
Place of Strength

The Secret Place of Strength

Marie Chapian

BETHANY HOUSE PUBLISHERS
MINNEAPOLIS, MINNESOTA 55438

Published by Bethany House Publishers
A Ministry of Bethany Fellowship, Inc.
6820 Auto Club Road, Minneapolis, Minnesota 55438

Printed in the United States of America

Library of Congress Cataloging-in-Publication Data

Chapian, Marie.
   The secret place of strength : a heart for God devotional /
Marie Chapian.

      p. cm.
   1. Meditations. 2. Joy—Christian life—1960– I. Title.
BV4832.2.C5227   1990
242—dc20   91-26978
ISBN 1-55661-219-2   CIP

For Llolyn

MARIE CHAPIAN, Ph.D. , is known around the world as an author and speaker. She also is a Christian counselor and a familiar personality to radio and TV audiences. She has written more than 25 books with translations in over fourteen languages.

Contents

Introduction

This book was written to build and strengthen our souls in times of trouble and unrest. I write to encourage and ignite faith. God tells us He will never leave nor forsake us and that He answers when we call on Him. As we absorb God's words and press them deep into our minds, we discover ourselves changing, growing, and gaining courage that is both supernatural and exquisite.

God is first and foremost a God of love. The concept of a supreme being who is cruel and vindictive is a false, worldly view. Ancient religions were based on this bloody belief, and lives were spent in miserable servitude and human sacrifice in a desperate effort to appease angry and hostile deities. Today God has revealed himself truly: He cares for human lives and for the quality of life we live—in fact, He tells us He cares about every aspect of our human life. Every need is His concern. Every hair on our head is numbered.

God has not promised us a life without suffering, but in His love and wisdom He has promised to give us His strength for every situation. It is all important to be familiar with His voice. We must recognize His hand in our lives in all situations. The uncertain world will not give us supernatural wisdom, strength or hope.

The Word of God is a flood of hope. His sublime words of power and truth will catapult the faltering spirit to unimagined heights of strength and courage. His divine and holy thoughts toward us, formed into words, unite our hearts with His. No longer do we need to scratch the surface of the world for reasons and answers to our needs. His voice is a balm, a healer, and none other can soothe, renew and enlighten us like His.

"My sheep know my voice," He tells us, and so we stop to listen, to allow Him to permeate the deepest crevices of our hearts with himself and His love.

And in the miracle of His friendship, we are ushered into the secret place of strength. It is a place we will not want to leave, a place where we are forever loved and cherished—a place where we at last are our true selves, beautiful, wise and strong.

As we share these devotional messages in this book, please remember to examine the scripture verses included in each reading. They will capture your heart and enforce the power and sweetness of His word to you each day.

Enjoy. Grow. Be blessed and happy. We have come to our secret place of strength.

Marie Chapian

I Am Your Safety

He who dwells in the shelter of the Most High
will rest in the shadow of the Almighty.
(*Psalm 91:1*)

Dearest one, I am here
   to reach into your need, eagerly.
   Like a youth who finds a rabbit in a snare,
      I am here to free you
from the hunter's trap.
   I see all the dangers you are unaware of;
they lie in wait for tender flesh
   like yours.
   Yet your foot will never be caught
between their teeth
   because My promise to you is sure.

I promise to protect you.
   Stay close to Me.
I will embrace you

with safety.
I am your barrier against harm;
I am warm and soft,
    and under My wings you are secure.
The deadly pestilence and
    those anxious terrors of the night
cannot reach you here.
    The missiles of doubt
that fly at you all day
    will not hurt you.
I am your dwelling place.

Come live inside my love,
    where no evil can make you fall.
I have given My angels charge
    concerning you
to guard you in all your ways.
    My angels are with you
to hold you up in their hands
    in case you strike your foot
against a stone.
    This is My promise to you.

Psalm 91:1–14

I Hear You and I Answer

*Blessing I certainly will bless you
and multiplying I will multiply you.*
(Hebrews 6:14, Amp. Bible)

You have been waiting
    for answers.
Now you are stripped
    of patience.
You cry out in the midst of driving winds;
    you are thrown on the wings of angst;
sorrow pounds at your dreams.
    But I have told you
I would never leave you.
    I hear you
crying in the storm.

Above the voice of trouble
    I answer you.
You are to Me

like a jewel of finest gold.
Your heart cry is My concern.
I alone hear your deepest desires
    and every need.
Do not be afraid as you wait
    for the answers you crave.
But seek My word,
    My breath,
    the wind of My Spirit.
I will carry you to the place
    where you will find
    all that is best for you.
    As you develop patience,
My best will multiply; it will
    create itself in you again and again.
You will hear My answer
    as a pure, clear call
within.
    Open the ears
    of your heart.
Endure.

Psalm 91:15; Galatians 5:1; Philippians 2:5; Hebrews 12:7; Romans 7:22

Everything I Tell You Is True

It is impossible for God to ever prove
false or deceive us. . . .
(Hebrews 6:18, Amp. Bible)

I want you to know My goodness . . .

I want you to
    soar above the bad news
        and the terrors of your world.
    Come inside the safe wings of My
wisdom and knowledge.
    I want you to be secure
in My care;
    I am Truth,
beauty and hope.

    I create passageways to lead you

toward Me.
Understanding is the light
    above the door
    into My heart.
I tell you—
the joy of life is yours,
    and I do not lie.
I want you to drink from the river
    of My delights,
eat the fruit
    of contentment
and rest in My watchful gaze.
    Oh, take what I have for you!
Treasure My words.
Everything I have is yours. . . .

Psalm 31:19–21; 36:7–9; 119:105; Luke 15:31

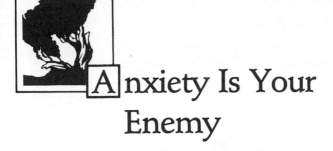

Anxiety Is Your Enemy

When your anxious thoughts multiply in you
    like mice chasing crumbs,
and when your days and nights
    are consumed by the fires of worry and doubt—
    pause for a moment
        and look for Me.

The constant gnawing of fear is more deadly
    than the serpent's fangs,
more ferocious than
    a hungry lion seeking meat.

I give My angels charge over you.
    They guard and care for you

in all your ways.
  They lift you up
when your knees grow weak;
    they keep you from falling headlong
    into the jagged boulders
      of failure
      which lie in wait like
      cackling hyeanas.

Your anxious thoughts are thieves,
    which are meant to trip you,
bruise and break your honor.
Don't give your time to fear.
    It's the call
of the jackal.
Be courageous:
    There never was a saint without sorrow;
    there never was a hero without courage.

Trample the venom of fear
and rise up and take your place
    of strength
        now.

Psalm 91:11–15; 94:19

I Have a Place for You

*I long to dwell in your tent forever
and take refuge in the shelter of your
wings.*

(Psalm 61:4)

Your soul will always find its rest in Me.
  I don't pressure you,
  cajole you,
  make demands of you;
I will never injure you.
  In Me alone
will you discover the sweetest solace.
  In Me you have complete acceptance
and understanding.
  You have a solid place to stand.

The world around you may tremble
  with confusion
and roar with fury,

but I am your rock.
Here, with Me,
    you will not be broken apart
    or shaken.
I have made many promises to you,
    and of this you may be sure:
I am strong,
    powerful enough to be your strength.
And you may be sure, also,
    that I love you.
I will always love you.
    I am your strong tower,
    I am your Beloved,
    and your friend.

Come now,
    and experience the peace
your soul longs for;
    take shelter in My wings;
take consolation in My love.

Psalm 61:14; 62:1–2, 5–7, 11–12

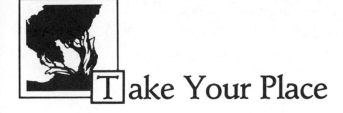

Take Your Place

You have given me the heritage
of those who fear your name.
(Psalm 61:5b)

Today is the day
for you to take your rightful place
as a child of God.
Today is the day
to rise up strong and confident
in who you are.

No longer will you mope and grovel
and allow the world around you
to play with you
like a plastic toy
afloat in a pond,
bobbing along without direction
without a safe place to anchor.
It is not good to drift
on the fickle currents of life
with no goal, with no light to guide you.

I am the shore; I am the beacon Light!
And I say,
 Enjoy the prize set before you:
 value your gifts;
be who you are
 with pride and dignity.
I have given you everything you need
 to be whole and strong.

Do not be blown off course
 by wrong assessments of you.
Do not grovel.
 Dare to be wise;
 Take life!.

Psalm 63:8; Philippians 3:14; Colossians 2:10; John 10:10

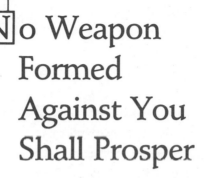

No Weapon Formed Against You Shall Prosper

No weapon forged against you will prevail; and you will refute every tongue that accuses you.

(Isaiah 54:17a)

When you dance on the mountaintops
   and sing the music of angels—
      when you eat the sweets of kings
   and ride the chariots of success,
      when your good conscience rewards you
   and you are unashamed to stand
      in the full strength of the sun—
then you will know
   your inheritance
   in Me.

Fear brings a strong person
    to his knees,
    and a weak spirit will swallow a person's dignity
as sand drinks the rain.
    But integrity—wholeness, clear direction,
single-mindedness—
    these are reserved for the strong.

Who reaches the peaks of high mountains?
    Who is able to describe for us
the distant side of treacherous cliffs?
    Who dares to climb higher,
press farther, endure the tempest of great heights?
    You can.
    Will you endure the storm?
Will you engage in the climb?
    The mountain waits.
Climb above the sharp stones
of trial and loss;
    invest in joy.
Refuse to give in to temptations
    and despair.
Renounce self-pity.
It imprisons you.
Your heart was meant to soar
    with joy.
Do not allow fear
    to capture your best,

to paralyze your strengths.

Keep climbing!
    Reach the heights!
I have a mountaintop reserved
    just for you.

Isaiah 42:11; 52:7; 55:12–13

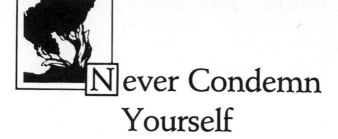

Never Condemn Yourself

You are forgiving and good, O Lord,
abounding in love
to all who call to you.

(Psalm 86:5)

You are precious,
never forget that.
　　Never let your soul
slip out of that sheltering word.

You wonder
　　if I accept you
with all your flaws.
　　Oh, I want you to know and like
yourself.
I am fully aware of each facet
　　of your character.
I know your choices.
And dear one,

28

I love you.
I ask you to trust Me,
to lean upon Me for your understanding.
I tell you to come to Me
with your decisions and plans.
I am the Lord
and I know your heart and thoughts
better than you know yourself.
But My ideas are higher
than yours;
My plans for you
are more wonderful than your own.
Your aim is too low,
your target too scattered,
your confidence is shallow.
Mistakes cloud your vision,
so I turn them into guides
to open your eyes of understanding.
The clouds of sin and self-reproach
waste your energy.
I know you are finding your way,
and I am with you to lead.
I alone know your soul
and all its ways.
I am God. Trust me.
Trust yourself.
I give you your breath
and number your days.

Be forgiven.
I understand you.
Never condemn yourself.

Mark 2:7; 1 John 1:9

Close to Me

But you are to hold fast to the LORD
your God.

(Joshua 23:8a)

The closer you stay by Me,
the safer and tighter you are wrapped
    in warmth and security
and the sweetness
    of our friendship.

The closer we are,
    the easier it is to accept being loved
and tenderly held and stroked by Me.
        Let Me remove the tears from your eyes;
    let My love be as a kiss to your heart,
        erasing bitterness,
    relieving hardness,
        and restoring sweetness.
    Let Me refresh you all day
        with My presence.

Examine the truth.
Identify the meaning of sin
    and do not allow it
to push us apart.
When you make excuses for sins,
    you allow a shadow between us.
    I have created you to live
free of the diseases of the soul.
    When you offend yourself and Me,
simply come to Me, talk to Me.
    Stand in the Light. Remember our friendship.
Repentance cleanses the darkening soul;
    allow Me to bathe you
in forgiveness,
    and give new brightness to your spirit.

I don't want
    the shadow-wolves of guilt
nipping at your heels
    and coming between us.

When you are close to Me,
    forgiven and clean,
you are fully alive.

Psalm 32:1–2; 1 John 1; Hebrews 4:14–16; 2 Corinthians 5:21

The Heroes in
Your Life

Remember your leaders, who spoke the
word of God to you. Consider the outcome
of their way of life
and imitate their faith.

(Hebrews 13:7)

Who are your heroes?
Are they true heroes?
    Today, make a list of those
whom *I* consider heroes,
    men and women of faith,
to be admired by angels
    and emulated by men and women.

I have put heroes in your life,
    men and women of strength,
courage and integrity,
    who demonstrate My steadfast character,
who live and breathe My personality.

33

Many consider themselves heroes
who are not:
There is no true valor
without humility;
no beauty of soul
without selflessness;
no glory
in vanity.

My son
Jesus
is your truest hero,
the One who gave himself for you,
who lived and died
in obedience,
so you could scale the heights
and find abundant life
in His Spirit.
The greatest hero
is the man or woman
whose life reveals
My heart.

Hebrews 11:1–40; 12:12

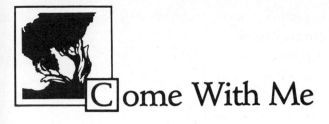# Come With Me

My lover spoke and said to me,
"Arise, my darling, my beautiful one,
and come with me."
(Song of Solomon 2:10)

Beauty
of days
pulsing, throbbing,
eager to fly higher,
to wear the garb
of fearlessness,
to strip the glue
from your feet,
kick the mud,
lift up the hands that hang down,
jostle the clouds,
kiss the stars.
Take the gift that is yours.

Majestic fingers
have woven a coat for you

to wear.
Streaks of light
dance from its sleeves;
precious gems cast beams of light
from its lapel;
sparks flame from pockets
carrying ignited answered prayers.

Rise up,
    rise up, I say!
        Put on the magnificent
        and come with Me.

Ephesians 6:10–11

The Shield of Faith

In addition to all this, take up the
shield of faith, with which you can
extinguish all the flaming
arrows of the evil one.

(Ephesians 6:16)

Arrows come at you
    like stinging rain;
they plunge into your soul,
    and burn smoldering craters
that no salve can relieve.

    Hear Me. Protect yourself
when you're in the line of fire.
    The thin gauze of undeveloped faith
will never form a hero's armor,
    and no war is won
without a plan of safety.
        If you know the One

in Whom you believe,
take all the power you can
in Him.
Take the armor.
Take the shield.
Take the intelligent plan
of strong defense.
Your faith is your garrison,
and your coat of mail:
No weapon formed against you
shall prosper.
I have told you to be strong in Me
and in the power of My might.

Faith forms an impenetrable wall
of fire around you.

Do you understand
how beautiful you become,
and how impossible you are to defeat
when you rise up strong
and with this knowledge of Me
embedded in the core of your soul?

Know the One in Whom you believe,
and, therefore, know who you are:

Invincible.

Isaiah 54:17; Ephesians 6:10; 2 Chronicles 20:20;
1 Thessalonians 5:8; 2 Corinthians 5:7; 2 Timothy 1:12;
1 John 5:20

Move a Mountain Today

I tell you the truth, if you have faith
as small as a mustard seed,
you can say to this mountain,
"Move from here to there,"
and it will move.
Nothing will be impossible for you.
(Matthew 17:20b)

Faith is knowledge,
    a gift,
    power.
Faith breaks
    the arrows of self-defeat,
    renders them pointless.

You—*you* are Mine!
And you must believe

and protect yourself
from the lies
of fear and doubt.
Believe in My love
for you.
You will
    overcome the world with its driving arrows.
You will spit the darts
    into a bottomless ditch.
Do not round your shoulders
and allow your head to droop.
See yourself for who you are:
You are My child!
Together we can move mountains.

*Hosea 2:20; 1 Corinthians 12:9; Psalm 68:35; 1 John 5:4, 19;
John 6:28–29*

You Are an Overcomer

*For everyone born of God overcomes
the world. This is the victory that
has overcome the world, even our faith.*
(1 John 5:4)

I have heard your strident complaints
 galloping across a landscape
 of disappointment.
I have heard the choruses
 of your mournful laments
in the long, weary hours
 of lonely regret.
The winds and dust of life have
 whipped at your eyes . . .
and I have loved you.

  I have always loved you
   as I love you right now.

Let Me teach you to live in health.
    Let Me feed you
    with the sanity of faith.
Let Me kiss your eyes,
    and restore your spiritual vision
    so you may see higher things.
Let Me teach you a new sweet song
    to sing to your troubled heart
and the world.

Will you allow sorrow, suffering, trouble
    to dig into your back like bricks,
    to hobble your faith,
    crush your dreams?
Or will you rise up,
        strong as the dawn,
        beautiful as pure light,
        brave as thunder?
    Oh beloved one,
        admit your weaknesses,
    do not be afraid of them.
        But seize the reins of faith,
            and overcome.

Matthew 9:29–30; Mark 9:23; Psalm 33:3; Revelation 2:7

Who Is Your Real Enemy?

Everything that does not come from faith is sin.

(Romans 14:23b)

Who is your real enemy?
    Listen,
your most fearsome adversary
    is not the world,
not trial, not sorrow,
not people,
    but your lack of faith.
Without faith
        you are a helpless soldier,
        alone, without a weapon,
        in the center of a siege.

An enemy lives within you:
    the enemy of your success,
    and your joy;

an enemy who steals
your gift of loving
    and being loved.
It's not "life," My dear,
    not circumstances,
        not Me.
        It's you.
        You are the only one
who can make decisions
    for your heart.
Invest today in winning.
    Take faith.

1 Timothy 5:14b; Romans 6:8; Hebrews 11:1, 33; John 12:46

My Counsel—
Your Crown

I will instruct you and teach you
in the way you should go;
I will counsel you and watch over you.

(Psalm 32:8)

Today
I have much for you to learn.
    See the joy
        set before you.
    Take the crown
        I give you
        and wear it with the delight
    that only the godly understand.
Do not be held back
    by hesitation—
those fright-filled pauses
    you call caution.
I give you confidence,
        surety,

a new personal bearing
    that raises your shoulders
and lifts your chin.
I give strength
    to your step.
I bless the words
    of your mouth.
    Wisdom will pour
        from you.
You are wearing My purposes,
    My plans.

Do not concern yourself
    with temporary losses.
The counsel of the Lord
    is eternal:
    See the permanent.
    Love the permanent.

Psalm 23:6; 103:4; Proverbs 14:18; 1 Kings 18:21;
Romans 8:28

Missing No Good Thing

Those who seek the LORD
lack no good thing.
(Psalm 34:10b)

Seek all that lives, moves,
    and breathes,
inspiring beauty
    in your world.
Accept only the lovely,
    the true, the comforting,
    the good.
Seek Me; seek goodness.
    Then you will stand bold and bright
    against the dark.

Does the sunset make excuses
    for the dawn?
Does a summer rain
    confound the lilies of the field?

Does the ocean evaporate
at the mention of a desert?
No, all things I have created
live and move and have their being
in a harmony
orchestrated by Me.
In my economy
nothing is missing.
Nothing is out of place.
I have created all things
in their time,
and for an appointed purpose.
The cactus,
the scorpion,
the rose,
the dove,
goodness
and struggle—
all is in order,
all is in its place.

Philippians 4:8; Ecclesiastes 3:1; Romans 14:16

Find Yourself

For whoever finds me finds life.
(Proverbs 8:35a)

You are accustomed to seeking yourself
in others,
    in achievements and labors
and in diversions
    unsuitable for you.
If you do not see My goodness
in you,
    you will always be unsatisfied with your life
and searching for the unattainable.
    You are who you are,
as I have made you,
    and in Me you will not want
for any good thing.
    I feed the spider, I feed the porpoise,
I protect the hawk and the sparrow,
    and I watch over you.
I give you *good*.
    I create goodness

in you.
Find Me
and you will find
yourself.

2 Chronicles 6:41; 2 Thessalonians 1:11

I Love to Do Good for You

I will rejoice in doing them good
and I will assuredly plant them in this land
with all my heart and soul.

(Jeremiah 32:41)

To be one with you like this,
    My child,
    to hear words of praise
from so true a heart,
    to know these glowing moments
    when you and I
are loving, captivated, engaged in perfect
    communion—
this is the purpose of My Son's death
    on the cross.
He is the link between us;
    He who opened heaven's walls
to let you enter in.
    Take in My Word:

Taste, eat, see and know
the heart and mind of God.
   I am the One
   who formed you,
and breathes breath into your nostrils.
   I love to accomplish good for you:
I give you opportunities like shining halos;
   take them and be blessed with good.
I also give you
   challenges,
unleashed from a sanctuary of bees.
   Meet them fearlessly
because you wear divine protection.
   I give you
   the opportunity to know Me
and to bless Me,
   and this is good.
Take the opportunity now
   to bring to Me,
like delicacies on a platter,
   the joy
the angels love to see,
   the joy you were born
to know.
   Come now,
let Me hold you near
   and give you good.

Come now, beloved,
let Me kiss your heart
and give you My best.

John 15:4; Psalm 31:19; Nehemiah 8:10; Jeremiah 23:23

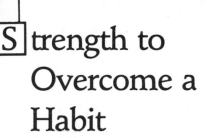

Strength to Overcome a Habit

*O my Strength, I will watch and give heed
to You and sing praises; for God is my
defense—
my protector and high tower. My God in
His mercy and steadfast love will meet
me. . . .*
(Psalm 59:9–10a, Amp. Bible)

The abilities I have placed
    within you
are stronger than your weaknesses.
You need not be
overwhelmed.
    My strengths in you
are mightier than
a screaming coastal hurricane
that transforms

a gently rolling ocean
into a trampling beast
charging at the land
like millions of confused
and raging elephants.
You have the strength
     of a hurricane
to eliminate
     doubt, fear, misery,
     loss, anger, depression.
My strength overwhelms
     all evil in its way;
     the waters roar
and swallow everything terrible
     in its path.
The strength within you
     is great enough to end the evil
     you have done yourself,
powerful enough to say no to a habit
     that would destroy you,
and big enough
     to erase all stains of shame.

     You can end the storm,
you can destroy the tyrants
     in your path.

So take your power
    and do it.

*2 Corinthians 12:9; Luke 8:25; Acts 10:38; Isaiah 1:18;
Revelation 2:7*

The Gift of Strength

O my Strength, I sing praise to you;
you, O God, are my
fortress, my loving God.

(Psalm 59:17)

When you ask for help
    I am there.
When you need strength
    I am there.
I want to see you live in godly strength,
and less in hungrily seeking miracles.

    There is one miracle you need now:
the miracle of inner strength.

    When you are strong
you possess all things—
dignity, solid footing, worth, vision.

    Be strong, dear one!
Be strong in My strength,
    and discover that new worlds

are waiting for you.

Yes, there is
new health, new wisdom,
   new understanding,
new success
   ahead for you.
With strength you cannot fail.
   I am in you.
and I am not weak.

Psalm 91:14–16; Ephesians 3:16; 2 Corinthians 12:9–10

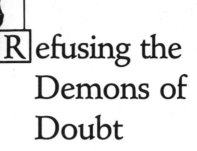

Refusing the Demons of Doubt

And do not set your heart on what you will
eat or drink; do not worry about it.
(Luke 12:29)

Ferocious turmoil
    like a stew of wild cats
screaming at once,
    clawing at the air
and raking their nails
    in the fire.
Frantic. Mad. Sleepless.
    Tearing the heart
with hot tears,
    sobbing,
What, oh what shall I do?

    Tell Me, dear one,
do you find answers
    in such turbulence?
Do you multiply
    your blessings with such
anxious moments?
When you wring your hands,
    does gold splash down from heaven
to pay your bills and
    buy your food?
Are you a happier person
    because you know how to worry?

Won't you calm
    your seething heart?
Won't you lean into the safety
    of My promises
and tell yourself
    to be strong,
Have dignity,
    you are not alone, because
        in your need
    I am there,
        and I will not let you fall
    into the abyss
        of your own fear.

Place your heart in My hands,
     for where your heart is,
          there you will find treasure.

Luke 12:15, 22–34

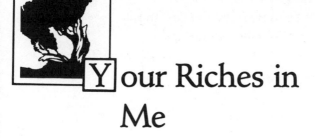

Your Riches in
Me

If that is how God clothes the grass
of the field, which is here today,
and tomorrow is thrown into the fire,
how much more will he clothe you,
O you of little faith!
Life is more than food, and the body
more than clothes.

(Luke 12:28, 23)

Be rich in Me.
  Be treasure-laden,
wear spiritual finery:
    take wisdom, humility, love, goodness.

Possess
    the gem of wisdom,
polished and lacquered.
  Be garbed in the opulent clothing
of intelligence

and wise choices
embroidered with the golden strands
of patience and suffering.

Wear on your hands
the precious stones
of humility and trials overcome.
Let the radiance
of goodness and mercy
rest on your forehead.

And let your words be
as diamonds of love,
falling like rain,
nurturing and transforming
with brightness
all they touch.

Be an encouraging one.
Let your hands, reaching to the
splendor of God,
drip with majesty, and
sparkling clean and mighty
to hold and help those
in unlit holes of despair.
You need never know spiritual hunger again,
dear one,
because there is no greater desire

than your hunger for Me.
And as I adorn and fill you within,
    you are free
    from hell and doubt.
In this world
you may be naked and poor,
    but I will make you
the richest soul in My Kingdom.
    I alone make rich,
and in Me the riches are from
    everlasting to everlasting;
they cannot fade or tarnish.
        Come, be filled,
take your riches,
    take your high position.
        Take.

*Psalm 45:13; 63:5; James 5:11; Isaiah 11:2; 58:11; John 6:63;
Matthew 5:6; Revelation 7:16*

Your Doubts Are Killing You

[Jesus] said to them, "Why are you troubled, and why do doubts rise in your minds?"

(Luke 24:38)

Bubbling, bubbling,
like boiling spoiled fish
smelling foul,
frothing and putrid,
spilling over
on all you do
are your doubts.
Will you let go of your
double mind
about Me?—
The constant questions
about the reality

of My power and
all-goodness?
Your doubts are
drowning you
in their stinking
soup.
Unhappiness and
instability
are the spices that
pepper this pot.
Is this what you really want?
Are you nourished?
     Come, starve your doubts
and be fed
          by Me.

Hebrews 10:38

 # I Am Faithful

Like rain that cannot fall
    upward
like wind that caresses the earth;
    like shifting sand dunes,
tossing seas,
    air to breathe,
so is My faithfulness to you
    forever.
Teach your ears to hear
    the constant songs
I sing to you.
    Teach your eyes to see
the endless blessings
    I have for you.
Teach your thoughts
    to embrace the truth

of Who I am,
   and why I love you.
Be enthralled with
   My ability
to change everything in you that is
   arid and waste.
Be full of assurance;
   be washed afresh
with confidence.
   I am here
and I am faithful
   to you.

Hebrews 11:6; 13:8; James 1:16

 Am Your Sun
and Shield

For the LORD God is a sun and shield;
the LORD bestows favor and honor.
(Psalm 84:11a)

Do you need direction today?
　　Is it necessary for you
to make important decisions?
　　Are you confident of your choices?

Trust the wisdom
　　that I have placed in you.
I have given you My Spirit
　　to guide and help you.

My Spirit is the penetrating sun
　　to burn through darkness,
My Spirit, by My Word,
　　is a light unto your feet

and a lamp for your path,
    ever-present in all your decisions.
My Spirit
    forges a path in the wilderness
of doubt and confusion;
    I am your destiny.

Do you need protection
    and safety today?
    I go before you
as a wall of fire
    protecting you from
        yourself—
    from the mistakes that crush
    and choices that confound.
    I protect you
from the deadly serpents
    along the road,
and from the power of the
    roaring lion.
    I am your shield.

Be prepared today.
    Be wise.
Take with you the knowledge
    of My glory
    and the confidence

of My favor.
    No good thing
will I withhold from you.

*Psalm 85:8; 119:105; 1 Corinthians 2:13; 1 Peter 5:8;
Psalm 23:5*

Your Reward

The LORD will guide you always;
he will satisfy your needs in a sun-scorched
land,
and will strengthen your frame.
You will be like a well-watered garden,
like a spring whose waters never fail.
(Isaiah 58:11)

Your hand, dearest one—
    I reach for
your precious hand.
    Yes, give it to Me.
Let Me lead you, help you.

    Have you chosen to
help those who are hurting
    and oppressed?
Look upon Me with your face.
    See the arms of God
outstretched to you
    as you pray for captive souls to

break the chains of sin and despair
in hurting lives.
    I am with you
as you share your bread
    with the hungry,
as you give shelter to the homeless.
    I am with you
in the loving care you pour out
    for your own loved ones.
Your righteousness
    shall go before you,
and the light within you
    shall break forth like the dawn
for all to see.

    I rejoice in you,
My servant,
    as you selflessly
give and share;
    it is then
My empowering gifts
    are put to use
        because you choose to be strong
            and not weak,
because you choose My power and might,
        not relying
        upon your abilities
        alone,

because you have loved Me
    and raised
your voice in secret worship,
    you generate the beauty
that demonstrates to many
    the reality of My love.
I promise you
    that the wounded
    and scorched places
of your life
    will be scorched no more.
You will blossom like a fertile plain.

Yes, though you pour out
    your soul for others,
your bones will be strong again.
    You will be like a watered garden
and a crystal spring whose waters
    never run dry.
You will rebuild
    all that you now see ruined
by godlessness
    and rebellion.
You will be called
    the repairer of the breach,
and I will delight in you
    and you in Me.
    And you shall ride

on the heights of the earth.
I have said it
 and it is so.

Isaiah 58:1–14

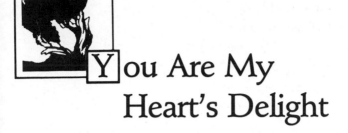

You Are My Heart's Delight

As the bridegroom rejoices over the bride,
so your God will rejoice over you.
(Isaiah 62:5b, NASB)

When you feel forsaken,
    remember I will not let you fall,
    will not let you hurt yourself,
    will never leave you alone.
Your courage wanes, and
your strength diminishes,
    but I empower you,
    I give you ability to rise up
    new,
    tough,
    beautiful,
    and pure.
        I heal you,
        encircle you in light
        and love.

I rejoice over you.
And there will no longer
be heard from you
    the voice of weeping
    and the sound of crying.
You are blessed of Me,
and My heart's delight.

Joshua 1:5; Jeremiah 30:17; 1 John 1:5–7; Isaiah 65:19

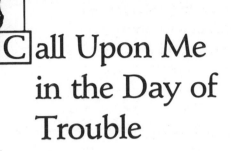

Call Upon Me in the Day of Trouble

Call upon me in the day of trouble;
I shall rescue you. . . .
(Psalm 50:15a, NASB)

Every creature of the forest
    is Mine;
the cattle on a thousand hills
    are Mine;
I know every bird of the mountains;
    everything that moves
in the field
    is Mine;
they are with Me
    and in My mind,
    beneath My careful watch.
The world is Mine
    and all it contains.

Am I unable to answer you?
I know the day of trouble.
    I know the day of triumph.
I form all of your days.
    I cause the dawn
    and the dusk.

I am the reason
    for all there is.
And I call you
continually
    to the luminous sanctuary
of My loving heart,
where you will find
    your reflection.
    I feel your joy;
    I carry your pain.

    Can you trust Me
in your day of need?
    Can you believe that your face
is always before Me?
    Call upon Me,
I will answer you!

And you shall honor
and glorify Me.

It is My joy and glory
to answer your prayers.

Psalm 50:1–2, 11–15

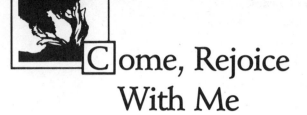

Come, Rejoice With Me

I have told you these things that My joy and delight may be in you, and that your joy and gladness may be full measure and complete and overflowing.

(John 15:11, Amp. Bible)

I am a joyful God.
　　I am not weak,
weepy
　　or morose.
No, I am
　　the God of all there is,
possessing joy eternal.
　　I sing, I laugh, I dance—
I am ecstasy.
I am joy.
　　Come, press My love,
like warm skin,
　　close to your ear.

Hear My exhilarated heartbeat
    and be captivated
by My love.
    Sit near to Me,
talk with Me.
    I listen to your suffering,
I know your patience,
    and I am pleased with you.
Come now,
    touch My ear
with the sweet joyful
    sound of your voice.
Because all is in My care,
    let us rejoice together.
All is well.

Psalm 126:2; Isaiah 12:3; 1 Peter 1:8; 4:13

Desire Me

O God, You are my God; earnestly will I
seek You; my inner self thirsts for You, my
flesh longs and is faint for you,
in a dry and weary land,
where no water is.
(Psalm 63:1, Amp. Bible)

You have looked and beheld
My mercy in times of disaster.
You have huddled into
    My warmth and comfort
when the days were barren and cold.
    You have eaten
My bread of life
    when hunger nearly overcame you,
and when the needle-sharp teeth
    of loneliness bit your flesh.

You reached for My hand,
the friendship of the Almighty.

Together we have enjoyed
    fellowship beyond compare.
That is why
    I tell you now
to come to Me,
    desire Me.
Do not forget Me now.

Isaiah 26:9; Psalm 107:9; Isaiah 58:11; Matthew 26:41;
Jeremiuh 29:13

Through the Fire

We went through fire and water, but you
brought us to a place of abundance.
(Psalm 66:12b)

The flames
twist and scatter
against the walls of the sunrise
like tortured rags;
sparks shoot in every direction
turning to smoldering cinder
all they light upon.
You stand in the midst of fire,
thirsty,
hot,
nervous.
Will the flames char and devour you
or will they form you into
a messenger of hope?

    Will you pass
through the river of fire on foot,
    singing My praises,
wearing the boots of faith?
    Will you conquer the fang-toothed
demons of fear and doubt
    who spit their fiery lies
        at you daily? Dear one,
    the way
to safety and peace
    and the abundant life is
through the flames.

1 Corinthians 3:13; Malachi 3:2–3; 1 Peter 1:7

The End of Frustration

I will give you a new heart and
put a new spirit in you; I will remove
from you your heart of stone and give
you a heart of flesh.

(Ezekiel 36:26)

Fill your whole heart
   with My words.
Fill your whole mind
   with My intelligence.
Fill your whole body
   with My enabling health.
      Sing the healing song
      of contentment.
Then frustration shall not plague you
   nor enslave you.
I have for you a new life,
   a life of joy,
   creativity,

wisdom.
Grow, dear one, grow;
  learn,
  love life.
Fill your whole soul
with Me—
  truly *be*.

John 17:3; 2 Corinthians 5:17; Psalm 1:3

One With Me

You have made known to me the path of life; you will fill me with joy in your presence, with eternal pleasures at your right hand.

(Psalm 16:11)

I want you to be one
    with My son, Jesus,
        who is
    one with Me.
My son could do
    nothing of himself.
He told you,
    "The Father who dwells in me,
    He does the works
    that I do. . . ."
You have within you
the same Spirit as Christ;
        Therefore, I can say,
            you are able
            to work as Jesus worked,

will as He willed,
and to do My good pleasure.

Grow in Christ Jesus—
do not be afraid of happiness.
Become one with us.
I am delighted to give you
experiences of joy
for I am joy.
Eternal pleasures
are locked within
the relationship we share.
Allow your joy in Me
to grow
and watch your strength increase.

John 5:19; 14:10; Philippians 2:13; Nehemiah 8:10b

Stop Punishing Yourself

He rescues and he saves; he performs
signs and wonders in the heavens and on
the earth.
He has rescued Daniel from the
power of the lions.

(Daniel 6:27)

Those self-hating words
    you listen to
are like wild wolves
    ever snarling and stalking you,
    robbing your peace,
    pushing you from
        your true place in Me.
They spring out of nowhere,
    claw at your windows and doors,
howl until you're nearly deaf
    and mad,
and with their hot breath

92

steaming the air,
they make you sick and weak.
When will you chase them away?
When will you rise up in power?
When will you release your fears?
You must no longer
punish yourself for
the sins of others
and for fears and shame
of the past.

You must accept this as Truth:
The past is gone,
finished.
You are forgiven
and I offer you a life
in a sweet and holy atmosphere
of continual blessing and mercy.
But when guilt and shame
are habits,
you cringe again and again
with loss and pain,
allowing the wolves to find
their helpless prey.
But you are not helpless!
I make you crystal clean
and new,
full of promise

and crowned with blessings.
>Stop throwing yourself to the beasts
>of anger
>and to monsters
>of self-hatred.

Be delivered.
>Be at peace with your life.

I love you.

1 Samuel 17:37; Matthew 5:4; Song of Solomon 2:11; Psalm 34:18; Joel 2:13; John 3:16

The Snare of
Anger

Do not be quickly provoked in your spirit,
for anger resides in the lap of fools.
(Ecclesiastes 7:9)

The person who flares quickly,
    who flies into a passion,
will deal foolishly,
    will do the unwise and the harmful thing.
Never excuse such behavior.
    Unbridled anger accomplishes nothing of value.
It is the mouth of destruction,
    devouring you, and
    devouring those around you.
Hiding your anger
    is like worms in wood.
The wood will soon crumble,
    soon be useless.
Unacknowledged anger brings
    bursts of fury,

' stirs up strife.

The loose-tempered person
pulls apart the woven threads
    of sweetness and peace
that make life lovely.
    Make no excuses for the angry one.
Excuses for cruel words and deeds
    are as tiring and sinful
as the cruelty itself.

Listen to yourself.
Hear your words. Hear your thoughts.
    You will find that anger is not alone as
it crashes along its thorny path.
Alongside anger comes the horse and rider
    of discontent with its army of transgressions
    and deceits.
Behind anger is malice,
    with flaring eyes and
mouth watering for revenge.
Contention, frustration,
    inordinate self-concern
all march together
    to form a wall
between you and
    inner peace.
    Catch those devils

before they turn
    and trample you.
Do not take your anger
    lightly.
    I want you to be free.

Proverbs 15:18; 22:24; 29:22; Job 5:2

Listen to Your Anger

Everyone should be quick to listen, slow to
speak and slow to become angry.
(James 1:19b)

Come into the light with Me.
  Knowing you are loved
and safe
  and not guilty,
and let us look at
  your anger.
See it clearly.
  Listen to it.
Respond to the feelings of your heart
honestly, openly.

        Do not be afraid of bad feelings;
            face them before the sun sets on
        irritation, anger, rage,
            and they are tucked away
        in darkness,

swelling and infecting
your soul.
Facing your anger will reveal
much about you and your needs.
Will you dare to learn?
I will teach you to understand
yourself.
The teaching I give you
in My Word is wise;
it is a fountain of life
to spare you the cunning devices
of slow death.
Is it not like dying to be trapped
in the jaws of rage
with your insides burning and churning,
and your mind screaming for relief?
The anger you aim at others
turns about swiftly
and strikes your own self
so that you become the victim
of your own rage.
I have taught you how to reason
and understand,
so that emotions and passions
will not rule you
and overtake sound thinking.
Come reason with Me:
Anger is not evil

in itself,
but lying and ignoring problems
can lead to evil.
Avoiding the truth
leads to great harm.
Do not suffer needlessly,
My dear one.
Give youself permission
to face your feelings.

Ephesians 4:26; Proverbs 13:14; 14:17

Dealing With Anger

*But the LORD replied, "Have you
any right to be angry?"*

(Jonah 4:4)

Be kind to yourself.
Be tender-hearted,
    be kind and
merciful
    toward yourself
as I am merciful to you.

The wrongs done to you
    have hurt and angered you.
I know you have suffered
    at the hands of evil.
I tell you, darling one,
    these afflictions can produce
an eternal weight of glory
    if you let Me take your hand

and lead you
    to inner freedom.
You have the power to forgive
    within you.
The sin becomes like dust
that flies into the air emptily
    and evaporates
        in a swirl of heavenly laughter
when you forgive others and yourself.
The pain is temporary;
    the glory is eternal.
Let the glory rise within you:
        Forgive them.
        Forgive yourself.
        Forgive life.

Ephesians 4:31–32; 2 Corinthians 4:17–18; Jonah 4:9–11; 1 Peter 1:8

Addictions

No temptation has seized you except what
is common to man. And God is faithful;
he will not let you be tempted
beyond what you can bear. But when you
are tempted,
he will also provide a way out so
that you can stand up under it.
(1 Corinthians 10:13)

Craving pleasure
    and the drive
to escape discomfort,
    to conceal pain,
to dull harsh memories,
    will blind you to the blessings of strength.
If you hunger for greater and more
    euphoric experiences
    with your mind fixed on temporary delights only
you become muddled, lost.
        I want to give you
           a clear mind

like looking out a clean window.
      I want to cleanse your mind
          when you are unable to see higher realities
          and true enlightenment.
      Eyes stuck to the world
         and its fickle rewards
     will confuse you,
        make it hard to change,
      to start anew.
But I am with you
    to fill you with higher vision,
give you new hope and power.

What are your deepest desires?
    Relief from the harshness of life?
A place of safety
    and someone to love you
unconditionally?
    Oh dear one, I give you these,
and more.
    I build you up,
addictions tear you down.
    They feed you
the poisonous message—
    that you are helpless,
    weak,
    hopeless,
    worthless.

Addictions lie.
  Addictions steal.
  They give you nothing.
      Their honey-laced voices call you sweetly,
        sounding harmless. They say:
You deserve a treat,
a secret, private thrill.
Who will know?
Who will care?
Eat, drink, shop, smoke, take,
lie down, avoid the truth,
lie, steal, gamble,
lick up the vomit of dogs.
You won't hurt anybody,
you need something more
don't you?
Don't you?

There are many faces of addiction.
  There are religious addictions.
I do not want you addicted to Me,
    nor to religion,
    the church,
    religious rites,
    or sanctimonious behaviors.
I do not want you to hide behind
    a banner of false righteousness,
    believing you are better than others.

I want you *in love*,
   freely choosing, freely giving,
freely being.
   I want you to live fully in Me,
rejoicing and at peace
      with the world.
         I want you
            to understand in your heart
            how precious is
            each
            breath
            of life.
   As My child
   goodness and mercy surround you.
I am your shield, your glory,
   the One who lifts your head.
Take your freedom, Beloved.
Be addicted to nothing.

Psalm 3:3; 23:6; Matthew 10:8; Romans 8:28; Galatians 5:1

You Are Free

Count yourselves dead to sin
but alive to God in Christ Jesus.

(Romans 6:11)

Frustration
    will cause you to grab for
immediate rewards,
    will yank you down a slippery hill
    to avoid the slow, steady
upward climb
    of the unpaved highway
I have for you.
    Impatience makes you forget
that nothing in life is free.

The thief wallowing in riches
    pays for his booty
with his soul.
    When you face difficulties
and temptations,
    there are no quick fix-it solutions.

Suffering is a portion
    of triumph.
Patience is the muscle and fiber
    of spiritual power.
    See the challenge
of the roughest path;
    accept the time achievement takes.
Find happiness
    in the wait,
    in the upward climb,
in the struggle and the endless,
    thankless hours.
Let your soul expand and grow,
    not squirming out of problems.
When frustration is conquered
    and patience is
the blue ribbon on your chest,
    you will be ready for anything.
    Strong in character,
full and complete,
nothing will stop you.

Matthew 16:26; James 1:2–3

The Song in the Storm

Wake up, wake up, break out in song!
(Judges 5:12b)

The fury of life,
    and the fears of the day
may cause your throat to tighten,
    your stomach to flinch;
but I tell you,
    listen for the song in the storm!
Be very still, and hear
    the music, sweeter
than human ears can bear,
honey-smooth and fragrant
as valleys of lillies.
    You will shudder with joy
        at the melody
    locked inside the storm.

In times of tempest rage,

open your spiritual ears
    and listen for the gold-toned
nectar of perfect harmony;
listen for the heavenly voices in concert.
Open wide your heart
    and sing along.

*Isaiah 28:23; 30:30; Revelation 5:11; Matthew 11:15;
1 Kings 19:12*

Become Familiar With My Voice

And I saw the glory of the God of Israel
coming from the east.
His voice was like the roar of rushing
waters, and the land was radiant
with his glory.

(Ezekiel 43:2)

Can you describe My voice?

Listen for Me;
wait upon Me,
and experience the rush of many waters
over your soul
as the King of Glory comes in!
I am the voice
within the blinding white cloud,
within the thundering storm,

the voice that comes after
    earthquake
and consuming fire.
    My voice is great and covers the earth,
and it is also hushed and small,
    imperceptible to the non-spiritual ear.
I am the voice in the still garden,
walking the halls of your mind.

    Listen for My voice.
I stand at the door of your heart
    quietly calling.
Hear My voice and open the door.
    I will come in to you,
embrace you, and tell you
    wondrous things
you need to hear.
    We will share the feast of life together,
you and I.
    We will be one:
        hear Me,
        come to Me,
        open to Me.

Psalm 24:7; Matthew 17:5; 1 Kings 19:12; Genesis 3:8;
Revelation 3:20

When I Speak to
You

*My sheep listen to my voice; I know them,
and they follow Me.*

(John 10:27)

I speak by My Spirit.
   You hear with the ears of spirit.
Hear Me.

All things happen in their appropriate time.
   There is a time for crying,
a time for laughing.
   There is a time for sorrow,
and a time to be carefree.
   There is a time for plenty
and a time for lack.
   All your times
are in My hands.
   Don't fret over the thorns
in your side.

Be glad
that the power within you
    is greater than the struggle
around you.
    I will cause
the voice of My authority
    to be heard,
the majesty of My voice and the strength
    of My arm
will be known—
    because I love you
and I speak to you.

            My voice carves flames of fire
            in the breasts of your enemies.
            My voice shakes the wilderness
            like a shirt flapping in the wind,
                putting an end to
            loneliness and sadness.
            I will cause your good deeds
            to multiply,
and I will strip from you
the unnecessary and the banal.
    I am singing
over you,
    pouring My thoughts into you.
I am climbing
    upon the pinnacles
of your finest hours

alongside you.

Listen.

Don't miss out.

Experience.

Isaiah 30:30; Romans 8:11; Psalm 29:7–9; 139:17

The Cup of Success

But arise, and stand on your feet;
for this purpose I have appeared to you,
to appoint you a minister and a witness
not only to the things which you have seen,
but also to the things in which I will appear
to you.

(Acts 26:16, NASB)

My Words
    are not mere sounds
and ideas,
    they are alive.
Each syllable
    breathed from My holy lips
instantly becomes their meaning.
    My words bring worlds into
being.
    My words *become*.

Listen for
    the word I speak to you.

You are *strong* I tell you.
    I have said it, it is so.
My word infuses you
    with power and ability
that can never be removed.
    You are strong.
    My servants who hear My voice,
who believe and trust Me,
    are golden threads in the fabric
of My will.
    There is no higher call.

            Travel your own Damascus road,
                even as My servant of old.
            Allow My words to fill your cup today,
                and heal your spiritual sight.
            Sense My presence,
                My joy,
            My constant encouragement.
You *will* succeed at your task
    as I have planned it.
I will never let you
    plunge headlong
into failure.
    See the opportunities.

Take your success.

My words over you are
    forever settled
in heaven.

1 Peter 1:25; Jeremiah 15:16; 1 Kings 8:56; Ezekiel 12:25; Psalm 23:5; 119:89

Don't Stand Still

Now this I say, he who sows sparingly
shall also reap sparingly; and he who sows
bountifully shall also reap bountifully.
(2 Corinthians 9:6, NASB)

A bird of flight,
    a rabbit running,
a skittering insect.
    Behold, all of life
moves.
    Leaves in trees bristle
and flutter,
    then float downward
to the earth. The clouds
    jostle the landscape of the sky,
and the wind moves like
    restless fringes across the earth.
All that lives moves.

Even the smallest cell
throbs,
    pulses,
        breathes.

But fear will paralyze you,
    turn your bones stiff,
and your breath stale.
    You remain inert and fret—
should you turn left or right;
    what matters is that you *turn*.
You want to know which color to use
    on your canvas;
what matters is that you *choose*.
    Birds make nests in your worries.
Fretting and standing still
    will never get a task done.
My soul takes no pleasure
    in the one who shrinks back
and does not act in faith.
    I cannot guide and motivate you
in the right direction
    if you are not moving.
        Move, I say!
            Be bold!

Dearest, are you worried
    you will make a mistake?

Are you afraid to lose precious time?
    Are you concerned
that your efforts may not produce
    the results you desire?
Do you wish you could see into
    the portals of tomorrow
to be positively sure
    you will succeed?
These concerns are vain,
    fruitless.
Your prayers will form
    stagnant lakes in your head.
    Your feet will be buried in weeds,
    your dreams wander like smoke.
        Awaken your mind!
            Take hold and move!
No energy spent in My kingdom
    is wasted.
No time
    is ever lost in a labor of love.
Remember, My rewards are
    not like the rewards of the world,
not temporary.
    I bless the soul. I enrich the heart.
I kiss the spirit.

You will gain only as you give and invest in life.

All life moves.

Don't stand still.

Hebrews 10:38; Job 12:10; Acts 17:28; Matthew 10:31; 2 John 8; Luke 6:38

Live Creatively

You did not choose Me, but I chose you,
and appointed you, that you should go
and bear fruit, and that your fruit should
remain, that whatever you ask of the Father
in My name, He may give to you.
(John 15:16, NASB)

You have been formed in My image,
    and this makes you a co-creator
with Me.
    Dip into the Source
of all that is life-inspiring,
    and be My hands and feet.
Create beauty out of ashes,
    discover joy in sorrow,
learn strength through weakness.
    Find the music in the storm,
see the colors of a thousand rainbows
    in confusion's murky gray.
Decide that life's simple treasures
    fill your purse.

Multiply blessings
and prosper
in the adventure of loving.
An act that is sparked
by love,
in love,
will always bear fruit.
Its fragrance will reach
far beyond
what the eye can see,
recorded forever in heaven.
Discover this.
See how creative
you really are.

Genesis 9:6; Isaiah 40:29; 61:3; Proverbs 11:25

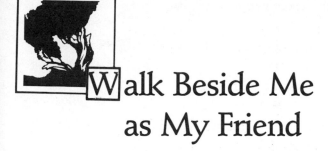

Walk Beside Me as My Friend

There is a friend who sticks closer
than a brother.

(Proverbs 18:24b)

The sweet ecstacy
    of union with the Almighty
will transform you,
    create in you a new heart,
elevate you above the thick fog
    of vanity,
set you free from the foolish pursuit
    of seeking your own best.
Walk in your integrity,
    walk with Me.
Iron sharpens iron,
    and I am the Friend
who sharpens you;
    I draw from the depth of you
where I have planted strength

for every worthy purpose.
I give you a heart
    to recognize,
understand and be
    acquainted with Me.
I am the LORD.
    I am your best friend,
and you are Mine;
    your whole heart fits
within Mine.
    Your soul, knit with Mine,
makes your presence a gift to the world.
    And more importantly,
you are a joy to Me.

Ezekiel 18:31; Proverbs 19:1; 27:17; Jeremiah 24:7

Secrets of the Heart

Jesus knew their thoughts. . . .
(Matthew 12:25a)

How far from Me
   do you think you can travel
with your wayward thoughts?
         I know your dreams,
         I am familiar with your plans.
         I hear the daily orchestration
         of your thoughts.
         You have no secrets from Me.
         I know all things.
I have offered to lift your heart
   into Mine,
to remove the pain and struggle,
   to cleanse the evil,
transform the past, renew the present,
   give you hope and promise for the future.
I am your future.

Hear My words
    and honor the God
Who placed the sand
    as a boundary for the sea.
Pause and allow the secrets
    of your heart
to run through
My compassionate fingers.
    Know My intricate ways,
My omniscience.
    Though the waves of the sea
toss and shake,
    they cannot prevail against
the fortress of simple grains of sand
    ordained for My purpose.
These are your holy thoughts.

    I want to be reverently worshipped;
Don't draw back from Me.
    I know your heart.
        All that you have hidden
            in the shadowy dark
        will be exposed
            in the light of truth.
        There is nothing unknown
            to Me.
Bring to Me your
    secrets of the heart

and I will create a new and
    wonderful world
for your thoughts to explore.
    Don't settle for ashes
when I give you
    gold.

John 3:20; 16:30; Acts 1:24; Jeremiah 5:22; 1 Corinthians 4:5

# The Cheerful Heart

The cheerful heart has a continual feast.
(Proverbs 15:15b)

When you groan in spiritual hunger,
    you may try to feed yourself
with earthly foods,
    bread, wine, meat, sweets—
but you will never be satisfied.
    Recognize your need for joy.

You cannot live fully without
    My perfect joy,
and My Son died on the cross
    to give you this gift—
found in tender communion with Me.
    Come feast with Me,
feast on our friendship;
    experience the delight
of the happy, refreshed heart;

    enjoy the soul's merriment,
laughter as pure as running waters,
    and know it is I who makes you happy.
My Spirit prepares
    a banquet of treats for you.
Your cheerful heart is your healing,
    your health,
and your privilege.

Proverbs 15:13; 17:22

When You Think You Don't Have Anything to Give

But Peter said, "I do not posses silver and gold, but what I do have I give to you: In the name of Jesus Christ the Nazarene—walk!"

(Acts 3:6, NASB)

What do you suppose blesses Me
    the most?
Did you know that without faith
    it is impossible to please Me?
Even more than your money,
    nice conversations with the needy,
kindness to the downtrodden

and wounded,
more than your good deeds
           and tithes,
    I treasure your faith.

A dollar bill won't buy
    deliverance from evil spirits;
a smile and a bowl of soup
    won't make the lame to walk
    and the blind to see.
But, oh, My dearest one,
    your faith will move mountains,
will heal the sick,
    give hope to the hopeless
    and courage to the feeble.
Your faith
    is your greatest gift,
    your most valuable asset.
From faith springs every good thing,
    giving you the power
to overcome evil.
    When your energy fails
and your inspiration lags,
    remember
that to do the work of God

your greatest task
is to *believe*.

Galatians 6:9; Hebrews 11:6; 1 John 5:4; John 6:28–29

Pick Up the Pieces

The end of a matter is better than its
beginning.
(Ecclesiastes 7:8a)

A tree that is cut down
    will sprout again;
it will bud and shoot forth leaves.
Even though its roots
    may be old and weary
in the dry ground
    and its stump dead and brittle,
it can flourish again.
At the scent of water
    it will awaken suddenly
    and green sprigs
will sprout from its dusty center.
Tender leaves, shiny and new,
    will emerge to meet the warmth of the sun.

Do not lie gasping
on the blistered ground of yesterday.
You are not in the mouth of a drought;
I have called you
to flourish like the palm tree.
Remember that death cannot produce life.
Life produces life.
Joy produces more joy.
Hope nurtures hope.

Now
pick up the pieces
of your life,
pick them up and look at them:
where do they belong?
Should any be thrown away?
Which pieces will you repair?
Do you care about the pieces
of your life?
Each new day I give you
the opportunity to drink
from the fountain of joy
and flourish like the beautiful
budding tree.
The best is yet to be.

Job 14:7–9; Psalm 42:11; Jeremiah 31:17; Proverbs 11:28

L ove the Present

Do not call to mind the former things,
or ponder things of the past.
Behold, I will do something new,
now it will spring forth;
will you not be aware of it?
I will even make a roadway in the
wilderness, rivers in the desert.
(Isaiah 43:18–19, NASB)

Never say,
"Why is it that yesterday
    was so much better than today?"
Not wise!

Sometimes you forget that
wisdom
    is your protection,
your partner in life.
    Wisdom preserves your days

and gives you
    good sense and wit.
Wisdom gives you My mind.

Wisdom will not allow you to lament
    the present distresses
and pine away for yesterday.
    I tell you to rejoice
for every moment given you.
        Be glad in prosperity
        and when adversity strikes,
          remember, I made them both
        for your benefit.
Do not live as a shadow,
    hungrily searching in the dark
    for a corner to hide
from the wind.
    Listen to your own words.
    Can you hear
the grinding, tedious sounds
    of your complaints?
These are like shadows, mere vapors.
    They vanish
with the shifting of light.
    Take substance. Take heart.
Take the blows. Take wisdom.
    Take life!
Honor today

as you honor yesterday.
The present time
   is to be lived
and cherished.
   Take the present.
   Live the present.
   Love the present.

Ecclesiastes 6:12; 7:10, 12, 14; Psalm 138:7

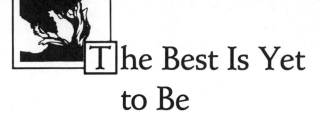

The Best Is Yet to Be

My beloved responded and said to me,
"Arise, my darling, my beautiful one,
and come along.
For behold, the winter is past,
the rain is over and gone.
The flowers have already appeared in the
land; the time has arrived
for pruning the vines,
And the voice of the turtledove has been
heard in our land.
The fig tree has ripened its figs,
and the vines in blossom have given forth
their fragrance.
Arise, my darling, my beautiful one,
And come along!"
(Song of Solomon 2:10–13)

Dwelling in the cold, lifeless
     sorrows of the past,
counting your failures and losses
     like beads on a string
will keep your face from Me,
     and the sun from shining
on your head.
     Your eyes will become accustomed
to squinting in the dark,
     and you will lose the desire to
change your circumstances.
     You will drink the wine of bitterness;
you will feel alienated and alone.
     You will fill your hours
with people and things to do,
     none of which can meet your
truest hopes.

     I tell you, rise up,
My lovely one.
     Put away the past.
Be at peace with yesterday
     and look at the
hope of *today*.
     I am beside you, calling you,
softly speaking in your ear;

I tell you the truth,
your life is good,
 and I will always help you
through the storms of the world
 as well as the storms of your mind.
I will lift you out of every
 oppressive pit
and self-destruction will not be your
 master.

When your feet become heavy with miry clay,
 I will pick you up in My arms.
I place your feet upon a rock,
 making your footsteps firm,
and I put a new song in your mouth.
  Beloved, look around you!
   See the spring of life.
  All is new, fresh.
   All is possible;
  all is ours.

Isaiah 53:4; Psalm 39:7; 40:1–3; 107:28–29

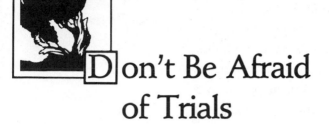

Don't Be Afraid of Trials

Blessed is [a person] who perseveres under
trial, because when he has stood the test, he
will receive the crown of life that God has
promised to those who love him.

(James 1:12)

They will come at you,
    sometimes like arrows raining
from the sky.
    Trials strike without warning,
landing with multiple hits,
    and I tell you
        get to your battle station,
           stand fast,
        hold your position!
Get out of the rain,
    strike back,
take the offensive.

    Never cower in fear;
endure the battle.

I am your sufficiency.
    I am your strength.
I give you the power to overcome,
    I am the embodiment of your success.
I am your ability in all things.
    I am not the author of your temptations,
I am the giver of perfect gifts.
    There is great reward
in facing your trials unafraid
    and pressing ahead.
Endure.
    Press on!

James 5:11; 1 Peter 1:13; Revelation 3:11; Galatians 5:1

Endure

Consider it all joy, my brethren, when you
encounter various trials, knowing that the
testing of your faith produces endurance.
And let endurance have its perfect result,
that you may be perfect and complete,
lacking in nothing.
(James 1:2–4, NASB)

Enter through the eye of suffering,
    like the narrow hole
at the end of a needle.
    Go through,
singing as you go.
    Don't avoid
life's difficult paths.
    I will not have you weak and pampered
like a fat rabbit.
    Exercise your muscles.
Feel the soreness,
    experience the pain.
Be complete. Be whole.

Be wise.
Be sympathetic.
Never be afraid
of the thief in the night.
Be prepared.
Your faith is your armor.
Your endurance is your
strength.

*Luke 13:24; Matthew 19:24; Colossians 2:10; Daniel 2:21;
Proverbs 29:25; Ephesians 6:16; 1 Peter 2:19; James 5:11*

Things You Don't Understand

How long, O LORD? Wilt Thou forget me
forever? How long wilt Thou hide Thy face
from me? How long shall I take counsel in
my soul,
Having sorrow in my heart all the day?
(Psalm 13:1–2, NASB)

I have
    always been.
I am the
    beginning
of all things.
    I am the
origin
    of thought itself.
Language, form, and
    substance are Mine.

I have given you things
   for which you never dared ask
   or think,
because I understand
   your thoughts before they are formed.

When you despair,
   you stunt your beautiful mind
and your thoughts become dwarfed and worldly.
   Let your thoughts be renewed,
and understand
   I visit the earth with blessings;
I daily load you with benefits.
   I have storehouses of goodness
   for you.

Sickness will not prevail
   over you.
The agonies of fear,
   competition, strife, jealousy,
anger, and lovelessness
   have no place at the table
I have set for you.

         You will not understand
            all things,
         but you will know

the interior of My heart.
And you will love
your place at My table.

1 Kings 3:13; Psalm 23:5; 31:19; 65:9; 68:19

In Times of Adversity

But he who listens to me shall live securely,
and shall be at ease from the dread of evil.
(*Proverbs 1:33, NASB*)

Pause, dear one,
and rest for a moment with Me.

   Allow Me to breathe upon you
with the sweet-fresh breath
   of peace.
Let Me enliven and
   invigorate
your heart and mind.
         Passing through adversity
            can gnarl your thoughts,
         deplete your energy,
            thin out your faith.
         But I will not let you fall.
I will keep you in perfect peace;

150

quietness will rule your heart,
and you will be strong.
   I will answer you
and bless you
   according to My promises.
Not one word of My promises
   to you
will ever fail.
      For this reason
         you must learn to be
      at rest.

Psalm 29:11; Isaiah 26:3; Romans 5:1; Ephesians 2:14;
Colossians 3:15; 1 Kings 8:56

Deliverance

Many are the afflictions of the righteous;
but the LORD delivers him out of them all.
(Psalm 34:19, NASB)

I remove the evil thing
    from around your neck.
I utterly destroy the weapon
    formed against you.
I strengthen you on the bed
    of languishing.
I lift you out of danger,
    and plant you
in a place of safety
    and contentment.
        Do not be so hungry for
            adventure,
      for easy affection,
        for tasty morsels
      that only vanish in the
        morning sun.
      These pursuits will entrap you.

But My Spirit,
    which raised Jesus from the dead,
lives within you!
    You are a new person,
a new creation,
    and you are delivered
from old sins and
    old habits
that sought to
    crush you.
            I give you a new life,
        a new name,
            a new hope,
        and an eternal
            home.

Isaiah 54:17; 56:5; Psalm 41:3; Romans 8:11; 2 Corinthians 5:17; Revelation 3:12

Loving With Your Whole Heart

Love the LORD your God
with all your heart and with all your soul
and with all your strength.
                    (Deuteronomy 6:5)

I understand
    your journey,
which has taken you far.
    You have traveled the wearying ideas
and philosophies of great men and women;
    you have searched and learned,
and asked many questions.

            Every step you have taken
            I have walked alongside you,
                loving you, calling you,
            wanting you.
                And when your foot slipped,

it was I who caught you.

   When the wolves of the night
attempted to devour you,

   it was I who rescued you.
I have loved you since the beginning.

   I formed you in your mother's womb.
I knew you before you were.

   In order to love your life
and to love others,

   you need only step into
the light of My love for you.

Accept. Partake.

   Be washed in My love
and the love that blessed you

   with talents,
with your body, mind and soul.

   Then you will see
the world anew.

   All will become miraculously
alive to you.

   Partake of the miracle.
Give Me your whole heart.

Psalm 119:2; Isaiah 55:3; Genesis 1:26; Ezekiel 11:19;
Ephesians 4:24

Who Is in Control?

Walk in all the way that
the LORD your God has commanded you,
so that you may live and prosper
and prolong
your days in the land
that you will possess.
(Deuteronomy 5:33)

What is the highest purpose
of your life?
It is to be part
of My ideal purposes.
It is to live safely
within the walls of My heart
all your days,
so that it may be well
with you, your children
and your grandchildren.

These are My promises
     to you:
If you will be changed in heart
     by My statutes and commandments,
you will prosper.
     You will know
great peace and contentment.
     You will not be continually
hassled with anxiety
     and frustration.
You will relax in the knowledge
     that I am in control.
          The secret place of your strength
               is to believe and trust Me
          and My abilities.
               Your efforts without Me
          are like dust in the wind.
With Me
     all things are possible.
     Have confidence in Me.
Let Me carry out My plans.

Deuteronomy 4:1, 40; 4:40; Hebrews 4:3; Philippians 4:13;
Psalm 37:5; Jeremiah 29:11

When You Are Searching for My Will

The word is near you; it is in your mouth
and in your heart.

(Romans 10:8a)

Do you want to know
  My will for you?
Are you seeking proof
  of My guidance?
Are you prowling the universe
  looking for signs
of My approval?
  Do you question counselors
and ministers continually for advice?
  Do you beg guidance from
friends and neighbors
  and exhaust your family
with endless problems to be solved?

I am the still small voice
within you.
Yes, hear the words of counsel
through others,
read My written words,
but then . . .
learn to trust the voice within
when you pray.

You will know,
by My Spirit,
if I am the inspiration
of your choices.
I am guiding you
in the path of answered prayer.
I am showing you
the way of discernment
and inner strength.

My spirit is unfolding
a living plan
within you.
There is sublime order,
intelligence,
and creativity
in My plan.
Listen for Me.

I am within you.
My will is smiling at you.

1 Kings 19:12; John 14:17; 16:13; 1 John 3:24; 4:13

How You Spend Your Money

*Why spend money on what is
not bread, and your labor on what
does not satisfy?*

(Isaiah 55:2)

I want you to respect the money
    I entrust to you.
Receive your money as a gift
    from Me.
Do not be careless with its value
    even if it is less than
you desire.
    Gain understanding
and financial integrity,
      and allow Me to prosper you.
        When you spend your money
          thoughtlessly,
        when you are given to whim
          and an urge to possess things,

you lose the sound of clear,
   holy guidance,
and your blessings wane.
Know that I give My best to you.
   I am concerned with
what you do with My gifts.
   One piece of gold or one million
are the same to Me.
   Both require prudence
and careful management
   to multiply and do good.
I want you to give
and invest in others,
   for this is wisdom.
      Humility multiplies riches,
         but selfishness diminishes
      the blessings of the Lord.
What is important to you?
   Where are your investments?
How are you spending your money?

Genesis 39:3; 2 Chronicles 26:5; Ecclesiastes 2:26; Ezekiel 28:4; Matthew 6:20; Luke 6:38; Acts 3:6

Be Yourself

For Thou didst form my inward parts;
Thou didst weave me in my mother's womb.
I will give thanks to Thee, for I am fearfully
and wonderfully made; wonderful are
Thy works, and my soul knows it very
well. My frame was not hidden from Thee,
when I was made in secret.
(Psalm 139:13–15, NASB)

Are you pleased to
be yourself?
Is it an honor and a privilege
to be who you are?
I want you to invest in your
self-awareness
because you will know Me
more fully
when you know
and appreciate yourself.

Listen to the song

I placed in your heart
　　when I created you.
Search
　　and discover the kingdom of God
　　within you.
Talk to your heart,
　　and be a blessing to yourself.
You will discover
　　the beauty of wholeness,
and your confident spirit
　　will touch others.
I would not have you needy
　　and crawling on the ground
for identity.
Walk tall.
　　Accept who you are,
and do not attempt
　　to squeeze yourself into
another's image.
　　　　You have already been
　　　　　　formed in My image,
　　　　therefore, be who you are.
It is *you* I love.

Proverbs 16:4; John 1:3; 3:16; Psalm 4:4; 139:16–17; Luke 17:21; Colossians 3:10

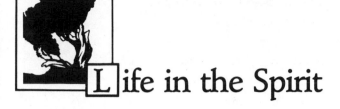

Life in the Spirit

If we live by the Spirit,
let us also walk by the Spirit.
(Galatians 5:25, NASB)

I have put My Spirit within you
    so that you may fully live
in My Word
    and enjoy the good fruit
of My Word.
    You know My Spirit
because I have given Him to you
    so that we may be one.
My Spirit and I are one,
    and your faith in My Son
has made you one with Me.
    I want you to live daily
in your spiritual intelligence.
    I want you to exercise
your gift of creativity,
    to give your all
to life.

The essence of God is to give;
and you are part of me,
    one with me;
therefore, you will be giving.

In order to be strong,
    in order to conquer
troubles around you,
    become acquainted with My Spirit.
Listen and respond to Him,
    for deep within you
He quietly instructs,
    guides,
and informs you.
    The petty concerns
that once felt like chains
    around your waist
will fall away.
    You will run with a lighter stride,
work with a steadier hand,
    love with a purer heart,
and think with a clearer mind.
    When your thoughts are illuminated
by Mine,
    you are walking in My Spirit.

*Ezekiel 36:27; John 14:17; 14:26; 16:13; Isaiah 30:21;
Psalm 143:10*

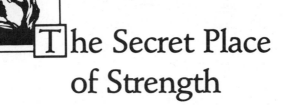

The Secret Place
of Strength

I have loved you with an everlasting
love; I have drawn you
with loving-kindness.

(Jeremiah 31:3b)

My treasure, My beloved,
    take My heart in yours!
How lovely is the dawn
    of your tender heart
to Me.
        I will be to you as the spring,
           with its fragrance
    and new blossoms;
          and you are My dear one,
        My friend and My beloved.
        I am the lover of your soul.
I love you with a love
    that shaped the universe.
I will help you to

ascend the stairway of joy
and gladness.
    I will give you the stars in the
eternal heaven,
    I will cause your feet to dance
upon the eyelids of sorrow,
    and you will sing songs
upon a bed of spices,
    the aromatic presence
of My Spirit.

I give you movement,
    wonder and vision.
I give you eyes to discover,
    hands to create good.
I am in you, and you in Me.
        I am the rain,
        and you are My forest of trees;
        I am the sun,
        and you are My garden of flowers.
        I am eternal majesty,
        and you are intimate with Me.
        I kiss your head,
    I bless your face,
        your body,
    your soul.

I am in you,
    and you are in
the secret place of strength.

Song of Solomon 4:7; Psalm 16:11; 19:8; 31:23; 90:1, 17;
Ephesians 3:17–19; 5:2; 1 Corinthians 15:54; Isaiah 28:5–6